Late Winter

Late Winter

Poems

Bill Brown

Iris Press
Oak Ridge, Tennessee

Copyright © 2008 by Bill Brown

All rights reserved. No portion of this book may be reproduced in any form or by any means, including electronic storage and retrieval systems, without explicit, prior written permission of the publisher, except for brief passages excerpted for review and critical purposes.

Cover Painting on Handmade Paper by Suzanne Brown

Iris Press is an imprint of the Iris Publishing Group, Inc.
www.irisbooks.com

Design by Robert B. Cumming, Jr.

Library of Congress Cataloging-in-Publication Data

Brown, Bill, 1948 Sept. 17-
  Late winter poems / Bill Brown.
    p. cm.
  ISBN 978-1-60454-206-6 (alk. paper)
  ISBN 978-1-60454-207-3 (pbk. : alk. paper)
  I. Title.
  PS3552.R68523L38 2008
  811'.54—dc22
                                          2008000590

Acknowledgements

Thanks to the editors of the following journals and anthologies in which these poems first appeared.

Alca-Lines: "In the Company of Grasses"
Appalachian Heritage: "The Shadow"
Appalachian Journal: "Epistle," "Grounding the New Millennium," "Remains," "The Bears"
Asheville Poetry Review: " Learning to Be Quiet"
Atlanta Review: "Soliloquy," "Table Nine"
Bayou Magazine: "Holy Shit"
Borderlands, The Texas Poetry Review: "Dream Letter Lullaby," "Fall," "The Language of Rain"
Cairn: "People Who Laugh too Loud in Restaurants"
Cliff Soundings: "Letter"
CrossRoads: "Tennessee Song"
Diner: "The Body Washer, Iraq 2006"
English Journal: "Driving through Kansas"
Karamu: "Threadbare"
Literary Lunch (Knoxville Writers' Guild): "Killing Chickens"
Louisville Review: "On the Beach"
Low Explosions (Knoxville Writers' Guild): "Diviner"
New Madrid: "The Elvis Egg," "My Father Comes to Me"
Mochila Review: "On Hearing that a Friend Has a Week to Live"
North American Review: "August Translation, Idaho," "Light and Shadow, 2004"
Now and Then: " Green Snake"
Number One: "Cottonwood," "Driving Home," "To an Editor"

Obion River Anthology: "Hill Top Ponds"
Oregon Review: "Last Rites to the Queen of Grammar"
Poem: "Genesis," "That Story"
Potomac Review: "Carolina Wrens"
Prairie Schooner: "And"
Rambler Magazine: " Language of the Hands," "With the Help of Birds"
Rattle: "My Mother's Soul," "The Rubber"
Rockhurst Review: "Tuesday at the Mall"
Slant: "Prayer for the Newly Dead," "When the Dust Settles"
South Carolina Review: "Lake Isle of Tennessee," "The Snake-Owl"
South Dakota Review: "An Absence," "Late Winter Longing"
Stitches: "What I mean to Say"
Tar River Poetry: "Baptism," "My Father Made Love," "Planet in October"
Tennessee English Journal: "Lilies," "Teaching *Hamlet*"
The Teacher's Voice: "Prayer for a November Morning"
West Branch: "My Lost Child"

I am indebted to Bread Loaf School of English, Radford University and Peabody College of Vanderbilt University for insight and encouragement. I am grateful to Humanities Tennessee for its continued support of the written word, and the Tennessee Arts Commission for generous Poetry Fellowships.

I thank Malcolm Glass, Randy Mackin, Peter Stillman, Ken Macorie, Robert Pack, and Ann and Larry Richman for early inspiration and friendship that lives in me still.

I am grateful to Parks Lanier and my dear SELU sisters Heidi Hartwiger, Isabel Zuber, Judy Miller, Darnelle Arnoult, Jean Simmons, Diane Jordan, and Tamara Baxter. Thanks to Kay Byer for her friendship, poetic example and support.

I am ever grateful to G'anne Harmon, Charlotte Pence, and Lola White for helping me shape many of these poems.

Special thanks to Jeff Hardin and Alice Sanford whose giftedness and goodness have made me a better poet and I hope a better person.

To my brothers and sister who so willingly allow me to tell our stories, real and imagined, and to my wife, Suzanne— my love, my critic, my best friend, and my hope.

—Bill Brown

Contents

Late Winter Longing 13

I Finding Home

Driving Home 17
Cottonwood 18
The Elvis Egg 20
The Literacy of Sleep 21
Lake Isle of Tennessee 22
Hill Top Ponds 23
Baptism 25
Dream Letter Lullaby 27
Sulfur Creek Ford 29
Holy Shit 31
The Rubber 34
The Snake Owl 36
Letter 37

II Breaking

Grounding the New Millennium 41
Light and Shadow, 2004 43
And 44
The Body Washer, Iraq, 2006 45
Infant, Collateral Damage, 2006 46
Threadbare 47
Prayer for Filling the Emptiness 48
August Translation, Idaho 49

Tuesday at the Mall   50
My Lost Child   51
On the Beach   53
The Language of Rain   55

III Mending

The Shadow   59
Epistle   60
With the Help of Birds   62
To an Editor   64
Diviner   66
Taking Joy   67
Table Nine   69
People Who Laugh too Loud in Restaurants   71
Driving through Kansas   73
Carolina Wrens   74
What I Mean to Say   76
An Absence   77
Learning to Be Quiet   78
Planet in October   79

IV Losses

Teaching Hamlet   83
On Hearing that a Friend Has a Week to Live   85
Soliloquy   86
Prayer for the Newly Dead   88
When the Dust Settles   90

Fall   92
Rummaging through Causes in the Museum of my Closet   94
Prayer for a November Morning   96
Lilies   97
Last Rites to the Queen of Grammar   98
My Mother's Soul   100
My Father Comes to Me   101
Language of the Hands   104

V Stories

The Secret Lives of Boats   107
Genesis   109
Green Snake   111
Oracles   113
That Story   114
Remains   116
Killing Chickens   118
Thankful Taylor   119
Back Home   121
Tennessee Song   123
The Bears   125
In the Company of Grasses   127
The Wish   129
My Father Made Love   131
In Praise of Winter Trees   133

VI Coda

Winter Wind Song   137

Late Winter Longing

Today, lapping lake water reminds me of homesick Yeats.
A crow barks a string of caws from a sycamore snag,

and in the background, a bard owl haunts the afternoon.
I am homesick for all the homes I ever lived in,

the morning and evening light that shaped our longing,
for the dead who go on dying, and the living who wait to die.

Out the window, rows of waves blaze in the sun, and though
this in not my home, just a lakeside inn, I am homesick

for the ridge rising beyond the shore, how little cedars poke
through winter trees. Another month and a shimmer of green

will brush the ridge, and a different homesickness will form
like willow leaves, reminding me of how my mother said willow

with a certain lilt, as if to catch its dance in the fleeting breeze.

I

Finding Home

You can never go home again, but the truth is you can never leave home, so it's alright.

—Maya Angelou

Driving Home

Driving back to West Tennessee,
flat wetlands and cotton fields,
giant gourds strung from barn
to house for swallows,
and this time no poem
will come. Hollow feelings
still in the stomach, nostalgic
loss of childhood, teen loves,
dead parents, all still there
but similes seem empty,
nothing worth comparing
to the loss, just the names
of things strung together
like gourds for birds,
or dead snakes hung
on fences, or crows shot
and lynched on pecan limbs
to warn others. Somewhere
in my memory a child
abandons broken toys
to make a fort with twigs,
always building walls
to hide behind, and an openness
in the sky cracks a place in me,
part hollow, part whole.

Cottonwood

—for Clay

Squeal of wood ducks,
alarm of crows
and the ticking song
of a king fisher's
journey along the shore
drift through years.

I stare down at the dock
in the river cove
and see my father
steer a john boat
transporting my sister and me
across the open water
to spend the morning
pole fishing from
a stone out-crop
while he trotlines
off the channel.
The sky owned the river then
and the bluff where
my mother fussed over lunch
in my grandparents' cabin.

What's lost, recalled
in little fictions I make
to shape the shadows:
my sister's bright face
whispering songs
to the complexities
of girlish solitude

and me, a child of moments,
content to hold the next one
and the next, my eyes and ears
filled with river, sky
and the hum a boat makes
puttering against the tension
of the distant channel.

What love brings me here
still holds with the drift of years
like cottonwood fluff
I catch in my hand, let fly.

The Elvis Egg

—for my sister

Our mother, like all mothers,
had spent Good Friday
sweating over boiled eggs,
dipping them in dyes: yellow,
red, blue, green and purple.
Some were stenciled with zig-
zags, others with dots and frills.
I was seven and you were nine
that Saturday before Easter.
It was 1957: No one would accuse
Elvis of being more popular
than Jesus, he wouldn't stand
for it, but that day he was.
As forty kids scavenged
the park for treasures,
you emerged with your basket
filled with bright candy and
hard-boiled eggs, your prize
balanced like the top boulder
of a pyramid, the Elvis egg with
"Don't be cruel to a heart that's true"
stenciled on sky blue shell.
You sang your egg to jealous
girls who squealed, swooned,
and pretended to faint, as they
swiveled their hips like the King.
You, my big sister, were queen
for a day, while sweet Jesus waited
in the tomb for the stone to roll away.

The Literacy of Sleep

In the Cuneiform of dry creek beds,
in the Morris Code of woodpeckers,

in lichen paintings on tombstones,
in a child's toe prints in cement,

not in the shattered windshields
of bombed cars, nor the shrieks of children,

but in the wondrous diction of sparrows,
in the morning prayers of pigeons,

in scribbles worms leave under rocks—
we are still here they say, older than bone,

older than the opposable thumb—
you still read us in your sleep.

LAKE ISLE OF TENNESSEE

May morning, power points run the university.
Bullets space-out data on the screens, students
at laptops finger notes. I drop the bottled water
that I found in the faculty lounge and recall a tin cup

and Grandmilt's spring. It burbled from a nook beneath
a cottonwood and formed the head waters of Cub Creek.
Like homesick Yeats, *I will arise and go now* down
Interstate 40, to the Parson's exit, cut the back roads

to Bible Hill where my grandparents are buried
in the Baptist Cemetery, and try to find the spring
behind the convenience store that replaced
my father's birth house. My sister and I played

in the dog trot, wary of the rooster who ruled the yard.
When Grandmilt had finished chores and eaten breakfast,
he saddled Nell and cantered us to the spring where
spotted newts cleaned the water as it bubbled

from beneath the ground. Wipe the tin cup with a cloth,
he'd say, jiggle a little water to wash away the dust,
be careful not to muddle, lean from the spring
and drink, he whispered, and we did.

Hill Top Ponds

Sleepless nights
a walk in any direction
leads to hill top ponds.
Like eyes they prove
what Whitman knew about
the learned astronomer:
knowledge can't demystify
but too much talk, like wind,
blurs stars on the water's surface.

I owe so much to hilltop ponds,
how gunmetal gray turns purple
then captures the first orange of sun.
The stillness of a heron hunting minnows,
a skillful stroke on parchment,
charms a human need for harmony.

When I was a boy, I circled
the pasture pond and crunched
frozen hoof prints with my boot heel,
trying to break through to something
unnamable for cloud and water.
Driven inward, I'd barter with silence,
offer up my smoky breath as prayers.

This winter morning,
my heart thaws from sleep
at the kitchen window.
A string of teal circles the ridge
seeking unfrozen water.
They find the large pond
on the Floyd place.

Cataract around its edges,
the center looms dark and clear,
a pupil reflecting a snowy sky.

In another month
strings of salamander pearls
will decorate the shallows
as peepers emerge to serenade
the mercurial mix of light.
For now, as day unfolds
may the teal keep their appointment
with the heavens. May a solitary boy
feel free to kick around existence.
May the county landscape settle
in the drift of ponds.

Baptism

Mid-May, the Gulf of Mexico
is layered with color, dark blue
where water meets sky,
clear green where surf meets
sand. Least terns soar, tread air
and drop into the ocean for fry.
Rudy Turn Stones
(what a name for birds)
congregate on the shore, run
the beach like wind-up toys.
Males display bright patterns—
white, rust and gray—their heads
harlequined with masks.
Soon they migrate north to
the Arctic Archipelago to breed.

My wife and I wade the shallows.
Thonged teenagers display like birds,
less formally, perhaps, as they
splash, strut, scream, and blush
at their own bodies. We stoop
in the warm sand and witness
two children practice baptism.
The oldest dips his sister toward
water in a serious evangelical fervor,
and says, *I baptize you, Margaret*
Jean Dawson, in the name
of the Father, the Son and
the Holly Spirit. He dunks her
with purpose and yodels,
rise up washed in the blood
of the lamb. We are humored

by his characterization—
excellent pitch, rhythm and gesture.
We barely refrain from clapping.
Then it's the sister's turn but
she can't lift him from the water.

Ghost is what my preacher said
that Easter morning when I was ten:
*in the name of the Father, the Son,
and the Holly Ghost.* Just out of
ear shot of my mother, my brother,
in his irreverence, whispered *holly
spook* instead, willing to risk
the consequences of hell. I think
he knew the creator has a sense of humor
in a world where beautiful birds strut
in mating regalia, half naked teens
flirt in the sand, war planes from Eglin
practice for Iraq, helicopters comb
off shore for drug runners
and children imitate their elders,
practicing saving each other, trying
to get it right in the long haul.

Dream Letter Lullaby

The night can't be harvested
like a row of beans, but like
an apple tree where you reach
up into a clutter of leaves to find

the fruit already punctured
by a wasp. Don't dishearten:
countless stars send their light,
even dead ones. Come back

to earth and seek the close wind
and the constancy of creek water
busy with stones. Remember how
your father's snoring woke you.

Your mother tried to turn him
on his side, comforting the dark
house with her weary voice.
That year of sleepwalking

made you fearful of sleep;
you awoke one summer night
in the fireplace, having dreamt
you were an eagle. Nothing is

more mysterious than the dream world
of a child. It hasn't abandoned you
just because you're grown. Open
your heart to rain, how it streams

a night window and collects
in little beads at the sill. Be as hopeful
as the hands of children sleeping.
Death is a sleep walk with an angel.

Sulfur Creek Ford

I awoke, imprisoned in a dream about my father.
Outside the moon commands the language of dogs,
makes a mammoth of the barn, glints the shoals
of Sulfur Creek below the ford. We were

coming home late at night, my father driving
the pickup that stalled in the swollen stream.
He cranked the old engine as steam rose
from the hood making the moon a halo

of mist above the trees. He shoved it in reverse,
then in first, rocking the truck back and forth
on loose gravel as water seeped in the doors.
The tires caught bedrock, and we backed up

on the road where we had started. My mind
imagined being swept toward the cascade,
my heart pounding, and then the moon broke
the cloud and opened the surface of the stream

like my father's nervous smile. That happened
when I was ten, and my father said that we'd
better not tell mother, as he drove the long way
to the bridge. He wore that crooked smile

at a thankless job, through the death of his father
and Uncle J.D. He earned a degree in chemistry
the year the depression hit—traded his dream
of med school to work the rails, then as a mechanic.

A gentle man of dark equations, at night he stood
under the porch light, a cigarette in his hand,
smoke rising in darkness, always backing up
and jutting forward, trying for solid ground.

HOLY SHIT

—for Clark

I

Predawn downpour, drenched
to the bone, my morning papers
becoming sponges, bicycle weaving
a wake in the road. I hear a chaooooga,
chaooooooga behind me as my brother's
baby blue Chevy flashes its lights.
He's saved my ass again.
We shove the bike in the trunk,
and I slide into the front seat to finish
throwing my route. He ropes a towel
in my face. *Dry your head,* he says,
as Blue fish-tails down Finely street.
I start slapping front doors
of row houses with papers,
my right arm sawing morning rain
like a politician in a parade. 63 houses,
two cokes and four donuts later,
we're left with the King mansion.
Tricky business, he says as he backs
down the narrow cement drive
with deep shoulders and cultured gardens.
Blue skids right on the slick concrete,
as my brother whispers, *holy shit,*
shifts into first, plows a deep trench,
pops the wheel back on the drive,
crashes into the wet street and weaves
to the stop sign at Elm and Main.
We're both laughing crazy, whispering

holy shit, 'cause we know there's hell to pay.
Though we'd been awake since 4 a.m.,
We cleaned up, put on khakis, Sunday shoes,
and waited for the phone call. By ten,
we'd helped the King gardener fill
in the trench and replant. Mrs. King
brought ice tea and told us to remove
our shoes. In the front foyer,
she showed us carved teakwood furniture
her father shipped from India during
the Empire. *Holy cow,* my brother said.

II

One morning before dawn, we were run off
by the sheriff for tossing rocks at the jail window
of the woman who cut her husband into chunks
and threw him into the Forked Deer River
as gar bate. Our world oozed with horror:
giant leeches, the creature from the Black Lagoon,
a woman buried alive, a man shrunk to marble size
being chased by his own cat. Our small theater
rarely showed new movies, but we didn't read
the national news. My brother hadn't left for Vietnam,
cop dogs hadn't attacked old people in Alabama,
and white bombs hadn't blown up little girls
in churches. Jesus still held his gentle head high,
and holy flesh and grape juice felt fresh
on our breath Sunday mornings.

III

How a brother knows to save a kid
from hurricane rains, escort him past
the pit bull on Maple Street, or cut him off
from witnessing the shoot-out
at the all-night juke on Highway 51
is still a mystery. It would be years
before I put my foot on the floor
to keep the bed from spinning,
or added to my trash lexicon, mother fucker.
This was my 13th summer, the last
my brother spent at home. He was
my night angel and *holy shit* was mine.

The Rubber

Youngest of four, aged 16,
the only child home,
I awoke one morning to pee
and found a rubber
settled in the toilet like
a bleached worm in a puddle.

Yes, I showered with my father
at scout camp, saw the wrinkled
pucker of his penis in cold water;
as a child, I spied, with interest,
my mother's nightgown cleavage
lead just shy of hidden nipples,
but for the first time
I discovered empirical evidence
that my parents made love.

Within months my father
would die of a heart attack.
Mother knelt beside their bed
praying for his life
in loud choking gasps.
My hands were busy at his chest,
my mouth at his mouth;
or I thought that I might
palm my ears to drawn
out her shameless pleas.

My parents were in their fifties.
I was the unplanned child,
a pleasant mistake my mother said.

The memory of the rubber
drifting in the basin as I peed
makes me smile at their caution,
their passion still warm
as they struggled to send
three kids to college
and raise a teenage son.
I flushed the evidence,
watched it swirl and disappear.

The Snake-Owl

Quincy and I skipped political science class
at the community college and, instead of
learning a new Dylan song on our guitars,

got stoned and drove the back roads
near the river, naming hawks. Marsh, sharp shinned,
coopers, broad winged, red tail—he called them all

by the way they flew or the shape
and markings of the tail. "Look!" he yelled—
crossing the Obion Bridge—as a barred owl rose

from shallows with a water snake writhing the air.
It was a sight myths are made of. "A snake-owl,"
Quincy whispered, and thus began the story

of the snake-owl we embellished all afternoon.
At Big Boy Junction we bought beers and baloney
sandwiches—mayo and two shakes of Texas Pete

is how he fixed them. Later we parked on the levee
and watched the Mississippi swallow the sun.
We had forgotten about the draft and our brothers

in Vietnam, about King shot dead in Memphis
a hundred miles south of nowhere, about a freedom rider
beaten in Covington and little girls bombed in a church.

As night claimed the river, we sipped radiant beer
and imagined the snake-owl winging toward heaven,
freer this time, dragging a chain of stars.

Letter

Wherever you are look up at the sky
and know the blue curve pulls over you

like a child's clean sheet to make a tent
of hope. You weren't meant to stay:

born to leave and leave and leave again—
never satisfied in a small town

nor a city, nor a shack by the beach.
For some, leaving is a new beginning,

for others, an end. Not like a tree
that tunnels its roots to claim one place,

its limbs reaching for its part of the sky.
For you, home is always somewhere else,

if you can only get there. It was a day
like any day when you left a message

saying that you were passing through.
Old friend, for once I wasn't home.

I had a reading in our boyhood town
where your parents are buried.

I left a rose beside each grave.
Too early you tried to own their sorrow.

Wherever you are, I hope this letter finds
you in a new place under the same old sky.

II

Breaking

In a murderous time, the heart breaks
and breaks, and lives by breaking.

—Stanley Kunitz

GROUNDING THE NEW MILLENNIUM

—with the help of Berry and Frost

Cutting wood, January 1, light snow,
the rich smell of split oak rises from
the ground where logs have fallen.
I pause to listen to winter, to feel
flakes hit and melt on my face.

A towhee scratches in the thicket
wearing a black and amber tuxedo,
white cummerbund, a fluff of down
against cold. This morning I could be
a ground feeder grubbing through leaves.

Most sorrow in nature, we bring to it.
Geese grieve the loss of their mates.
Elephants' strong memories honor
their dead. But the towhee feeding
in the brush doesn't think of his

certain death, doesn't carry death
around like a keepsake to be taken
out and fondled. Today, I slam
a ten pound maul to split oak
and hickory, to hammer the need

to grieve, to manicure kindling,
to mute the killing, to make chunks
perfect for burning. The six o'clock news?
"Stay away from screens," Wendell Berry wrote.
The snow has turned to bigger flakes.

They sky-dive like little hang gliders,
curving through the black maze of limbs.
When "life is too much like a pathless
wood," Frost wrote. But the flakes don't
notice as they flock branches, blanket

the ground. The towhee is joined by his mate.
He greeps a greeting. The labor complete,
I haul split logs to the porch. Ten trips
of stacking wood, of feeling the hard weight
press my heels into the ground, grubbing my way.

Light and Shadow, April 1, 2004

Down the hollow from the porch
three deer graze their way slowly,
chewing sedge and saw briar.
Spring trees stencil the forest floor
with spiky beginnings of leaves.
One doe's flank swims with shadows
and I am mesmerized by light.
My wife, who brings coffee and paper,
points to the deer and smiles.
I glance at the headlines:
nine Americans dead in Iraq,
charred remains dragged
through the streets of Fallujah,
two bodies hung from a bridge.
My grandfather fought in WWI,
my father in WWII, my brother
was wounded in Vietnam,
my best friend in basic training
died near Da Nang. I won't speak
against the courage of soldiers,
but sound bites and pictures
have haunted my fifty years
with wars that surround humanity's
neck like a string of death pearls.
Yet in the hills of Tennessee,
even on cloudy days,
the copper of broom sage
tames unmown pastures,
where the flight of birds
charms the pewter
of roadside ponds.

And

Friday, home from work, I flip on the war
and watch a group of marines help a family

bury their dead, and it seems that soldiers
called the car to stop with bull horns, but

was the driver deaf? No one knew, so the car
was destroyed, and the Shiah women

wail and wave their hands against losing
what they love, against the charred remains,

and the marines stare at their feet,
and one young man being interviewed can't

look at the camera, and the Imam proclaims
them martyrs, says that they are already

with God, and the sand and dirt pitch
from the shovels as holes deepen,

and the desert sun cannot prevent
the holes from filling up with shadows,

and the deeper, the darker they become
until the bodies are lowered and

the wailing and waving of hands
continue and one of the town fathers

lets the translator kiss him
on the customary cheek.

The Body Washer, Iraq 2006

—after hearing an interview on NPR

The body washer remembers her first corpse,
an old man burned beyond hope.
How could she clean such a one,
lay the white cloth over genitals
and scrub the scorched flesh?
The body washer's children would starve,
so she mumbled through the chosen
Koranic verses and knew that night
would hold visions of the dead.
Her calling came when a young mother
and her infant were fused together
in a car fire. The body washer
got permission to clean them as one.
Since the American invasion,
work has been steady, too many
bodies to wash, despite the gifts
from their families. She teaches
her daughters the proper way
to clean the dead. There is little work
for poor girls. She would not have them
turn to prostitution. You must believe
in a strong hereafter, study the Koran
and let the soul choose the verses to chant
as you scrub and herb the skin. At night
she still dreams of the mother and child
cauterized into one embrace, purified by fire.
You must prepare a white cloth to lay
the body on, and another one to cover it.
You must hold in your heart disparate verses
as if they were one. Dust, the only possession
death carries to the grave, is sprinkled
on the loved one's eyes.

Infant, Collateral Damage 2006

She has forgotten her mother's breast,
her father's coaching smile that made her

smile in return. She no longer points
when her sister says *Light*. The words

forming in her mouth are mute,
lost in the sand that for a time

will shape her features, then take them
as its own. Overhead, far above

the killing planes, above the satellite's
pinpoint aim, night lights cold candles

as if to grieve how easily joy and loss
intermingle like clay and sand and stars.

Threadbare

Were the mornings windless,
silent things that made your own

thoughts unthink themselves
and retreat into the fields

stolen by winter? And
the nights, who were they,

humorless pilgrims, wracked
with guilt? And forgiveness,

was it possible, the grace
you desired so threadbare

that speaking any name,
even your own, rang hollow,

the word open, without
boundaries, terrifying.

Prayer for Filling the Emptiness

The first rainy morning after weeks of drought
gleams like a child who wakes from dreaming.
Some longing opens a space inside,
and I feel like the old sycamore
that survives despite the hollow
in the base of its trunk. On the porch
rain streams from the roof into the Rose
of Sharon, drenching its purple blossoms.
Nothing much happens at six a.m.—
crows inspect a road kill,
and my neighbor's pony reaches
for a tuft of hay through the fence.
So much of life is reaching for
what looks better than we've got,
when the emptiness inside
needs another way of filling.
A man who chooses seclusion
learns to navigate silence, his senses
awakened to the hummingbird's warning,
or the way a fox tilts its head
to track a tunneling mole.
One can sit on the porch long enough
to learn the language of maples,
a language we forgot after childhood.
The secret is to make the smallest
acts sacred. Pouring a cup of hot tea
on a rainy morning should be as prayerful
as peeing off the porch at midnight,
humbled by a sweep of stars.

August Translation, Idaho

I saw desert sage give way to ponderosa,
great trees caressed by canyon thermals,
unmoved by snow tipped peaks of the Sawtooth.

I heard the mumble of late summer:
lightening's ascent and the shrill calls
of elk to their calves, of wolves,

stars and the surprise of rain.
This prayer must have heartened
marmots, night hawks, and otter

in their anguish over the hardening earth.
What I felt was unsympathetic and soothing
as blood draining into sand,

and coyote pups raising muzzles
to celebrate a kill, a healing-over,
like lichen on a creek stone or a scab

on a wound. And what I knew was
not knowledge, but ruthless and sensual
as ospreys saying their names to rivers,

final and endless as the flutter of aspens,
the drift of cottonwood and cliff swallows
holding back the night with wings.

Tuesday at the Mall

After the child who was running
through the garden aisle at Wal-Mart
knocked over a stand of seeds,
tripped on a sack of fertilizer,
forged head-first into a stack
of fifty-pound bags of mulch,
his mother caught him, and,
like a thug in a gangster movie,
hit him hard, and to justify her action,
snapped, "I warned you when we
got out of the truck." She drug him
by the collar to the back near
the lawn poison, and nobody,
not an employer or customer
tried to intervene, as she whipped
him in public, his stubborn pride
allowing little grunts instead of cries,
his hatred as red and powerful
as his mother's. When she brought
him back, cleansed of sin, he bit
his lip into a sneer to face our
turned down faces, our hands
busy shuffling and reshuffling
merchandise, all of us in line
at check out station three,
the light above the cash register
bright with shame.

My Lost Child

Stares from the arms of parents
in cafes, at the park. She grabs
the air and her papa gives

his fleshy hand which she tugs
into an udder for teething.
My lost child peeks out of papooses

wearing a railroad hat with a bill
shading her face from the sun.
She reaches out for me, her father

quickens his pace without looking.
I have heard her call from strollers
and front yard playpens filled

with bears and springing mobiles.
I have heard her cry through
thin walls of cheap motels,

heard her mother's sharp words,
and I have slammed my door
to walk the dark parking lot.

My lost child is frightened
by thunder. She gropes
the empty hall with streaming

tears and muffled screams
too deep to cry. She opens
my bedroom door and waves

her hands against this dream,
waves her hands against
the air she will not breathe.

On the Beach

Sitting on a beach in Florida—
7 a.m. and already couples
are walking the shore, some
let blue waves swirl their ankles,
others watch distant shrimp boats
or surmise the horizon at the edge
of curvature. I think of Frost's poem
about the shallow vision of humans
who see neither out too far
nor in too deep. To get here
we drove through a state
in which a preacher ordered
his congregation to support
the president or leave the church,
while in Afghanistan students
are killed protesting rumors
that American guards flushed
a Koran at Guantanamo Bay.
I won't guess what Mohammed might
say about the loss of young lives
over desecrated paper or whether
our Christian leaders wonder
if Christ considers collateral
damage a mortal sin, or what
Jefferson would think about
our praising military dictatorships
for their democratic ways
whenever they support our interests.
The sound of waves roaming
the shore is so calming that
I'll consider the ocean half full,
or even fuller, given polar ice

melt from my use of fossil fuel.
Today, I'll be born again like
our leader; after all, one definition
of faith is to choose to believe, even
when the world seems to be going
to hell in a hand basket. Who needs
good public schools when you have
the biggest bombs, who needs universal
health care when every hospital
has an emergency room, who needs
traditional allies that whine
about political solutions when
you can afford to buy new ones?
I recall a Holocaust survivor saying that
all disaster needs is for good people
to do nothing. *Turn or Burn,*
a sign warns at the inter costal bridge,
Are you ready for the Rapture?

The Language of Rain

How luxurious a forest after rain—
soft moss woven in the wreckage
of old wood, a gallery of lichen
on tree bark. It is winter—

beech trees cling to tattered leaves
to translate the language of rain,
to interpret wind. If you live among beech,
you keep something inside that listens

for that sound, that asks, did I hear it
when the fox stood at the mailbox,
or the day news pronounced the first
soldiers dead and flashed their pictures.

One morning I pulled a blanket around
my shoulders and sat on the porch to hear
rain and beech leaves make that sound.
What were they saying—nothing about

machinegun fire, sudden explosions,
burned-out markets, or a shoe
in the street still wearing a foot,
but something about the birth

of my neighbor's foal and the reflection
of the mare's eyes in the watering trough,
that between clapping leaves and scattered
rain there is a silence I long for.

III

Mending

*I need the words that are left
to go on searching for the ones I've lost.*

—Chana Bloch

The Shadow

Summer's old garden
is turned under,
a few green tomatoes left,
a rotten squash
the size of a melon,
the boy's shadow
stooped over
the skeletons of beans.

Winter can claim it now
that maples have colored,
and a skein of ice
circles creek rocks.
The boy won't mind;
beans stand in jars,
but the soil remembers,
sleeps with his shadow.

Epistle

Days before her death
my mother took an ancient
letter from a drawer
and read to me.

Her voice, though strong,
finished sentences
with a breathless sigh.
A distant cousin wrote

home on the occasion
of Robert E. Lee's death.
A great flood hit Virginia.
Farm houses and barns

swept the swollen torrent
like match stick ships.
Suddenly men saw wooden planks
held an infant as in a crib,

playing with a twig and leaf.
In a john boat they risked
their lives to save the child
whose identity was never known.

The formal nature of the epistle
was softened by the tale,
its voice miraculous in tone.
In my mother's marrow,

red blood cells ceased
to form. Her living will
said to cut her loose
from machines that might

prolong incapacity and pain.
At fifty four,
both parents gone.
I keep the letter close.

With the Help of Birds

> *For to come upon warblers in early May*
> *was to forget time and death:*
> —Theodore Roethke

Every poem of death
    should start
with my mother's love
    for birds.
Finches and waxwings
    her favorites,
though she wasn't
    one to quibble;
an eagle dragging a carp
    across the sky
would do.

There are worse things
    than being dead.
You might be swallowed
    by the daily minutia
of the great mundane,
    to be spit up
years later
    wondering where
your life has gone.

But loving something
    can save you:
the way finches
    stack a feeder,
meddle in each other's
    business until

a woodpecker crashes in,
    littering surrounding
shrubs with wings.

Last summer my wife
    found a hummingbird
on Mount Pisgah.
    Its emerald wings trembled
as its feet tried to grasp
    her fingers.
A ranger said
    that their lives
are so short anyway.
    What a curious reply,
I thought, but later
    reconsidered.
Perhaps any time
    being a hummingbird
is enough.

To an Editor

You ask me to put aside feelings
in order to see, but the wind
in the maple still sprinkles
the lawn with shadows,
glint on water is as magic
as alchemy, and everyone
I ever love will die too soon.
I know that my language
isn't really about how language
rises from pre-language
or whether feelings are based on
the urge of words or vice-versa.
I can write about a persona
in a taxi arriving at an address
where his lost daughter lives
with strangers, and he looks
in the window at people laughing
at a story she tells, so he orders
the taxi back to the airport,
flies home to a life of solitude.
I can jam syntax together so
the story can be deconstructed
and retold in, oh, so many ways:
how I heard the piliated laugh
through the forest while my
daughter in another city stares
out at traffic as my mother heats
milk at bedtime, never thinking
of my future heart attack, and
somewhere a child coughs
in a dark room and contemplates

her life, the lives of others,
their sorrows and joys, tries
to find words to fit them
before she is taught to hate
poetry.

Diviner

Walking across campus
near the law school
a student in a pleated skirt
and black tennis shoes
uses her white cane
to survey terrain
before her cautious steps.

My grandfather knew
a man with the gift.
He arrived one morning
with a smooth willow wand,
a dowsing rod, he called it,
to find a well in the orchard.

With the same grace
the young woman divines
the frost buckled cement,
the steps, the curb drop,
where she stops to wait
for the light to change.
She zips up her jacket
against December, straightens
the backpack on her shoulders,
speaks to an acquaintance,
laughs at a little joke,
lifts out her cane
in an even sweeping,
and crosses the busy street,
a smile lingering on her face.

My grandfather called
the diviner's gift the sight.

Taking Joy

> *You have to allow yourself to take joy.*
> *Otherwise, you are no good to anyone.*
> —Ruth Stone

Taking joy isn't easy,
as if you could ignore
lost faces on city streets,

or playgrounds littered
with broken glass.
Even so, some crone

wearing a crown of wrinkles
whispers to an ancient chow
as if he were Jesus,

or sudden mirth opens
a bum's crooked teeth
to see pigeons soil a saint.

You harbor joy inside,
afraid to loose it in a world
that doesn't give things back.

This October morning
brings hickory leaves
yellowed gold and starlings

flurry the park for crumbs,
their feathers jeweled by sun.
Perhaps the newly dead

won't soon arise nor the crippled
throw down their crutches,
but an old woman with cane

trudges along the market
clutching Sunday funnies
in her free hand,

whistling a song
that her first lover
sang in the shower.

Table Nine

Oh Grandmother,
while eating breakfast
at Cracker Barrel,
imagine my surprise
to find your antique picture
hanging in a grouping
with a Coca-Cola sign,
a stranger on a tractor,
and a mule breaking sod.

You taught me
how to tight-line fish
on Cub creek,
to spit on my hands,
and rub them in sand
to take an eel off a hook,
to steal eggs beneath a hen,
to suck on Hore Hound
to make it last.

Which cousin betrayed you,
hawked the portrait at a yard sale,
not knowing that you'd end up
in a chain restaurant
with an old-timer motif?

The last time our eyes met
you were in intensive care
at the Madison County Hospital,
hooked up to machines, your jaw
set against doctors who wouldn't

let your heart stop so you
could drift to your just reward.

Now you hang above table nine
in the non-smoking section,
honored or condemned,
I don't know, to gaze
at two eggs over-easy
with hash-browns. Rhonda
will be your server now.

People Who Laugh Too Loud in Restaurants

Nothing is as annoying as teenagers
groping each other in the front row
of a movie theater while the heroine
is diagnosed with cancer,
or a man shouting at his wife
on a cell phone while standing
in line to buy a hot dog,
or a woman lecturing her son
on the dangers of drugs while picking
through tomatoes at the market.
But people who laugh too loud
in restaurants should be charged
for the piece of fillet you swallowed
whole, the lobster bisque you couldn't
hear yourself sip, the Chardonnay
you spilled on your cheese cake.

I'm eating lunch in a cafe
when hyena bursts sound
from a table near the window.
A woman at the next booth closes
her eyes and grits her teeth. Though
we turn and look, the man is so
absorbed with his story that
he is unaware of the volume
or idiocy of his bluster. What if
he opened his huge mouth
and, suddenly, silence, just the wisp
that a chunk of baked potato makes
sticking in his wind pipe; then we
are pleasantly surprised by the
peace, until a four hundred pound

gorilla, escaped from the zoo,
shows up in time to give
the man a Heimlich maneuver,
but instead of dislodging the potato,
his head pops off like a champagne cork
and impales itself on a spike
in the ceiling fan. Just a thought.

Driving Through Kansas

A light rain softens a June morning
on the prairie. A sign reading *Yahweh's
Assembly of the Messiah* is one mile
from *Passion's Videos and Lingerie.*
Fundamentalist dogma and lust coexist
closely. Given the expanse of the landscape,
I imagine there is room for both.
Out the window, scissortails perch
on barbed wire, great tailed grackles
jerk at road kill, and a Swanson's hawk
circles in the sky. I won't comment on the sign
that says *The world's Largest Prairie Dog.*
But on the subject of religion versus lust,
I've always wondered about the fascination
with freeing the spirit from the same body
whose youthful beauty we celebrate.
Perhaps at 57, I understand a little about
the nebulous nature of the soul and loss
of the physical. This morning while driving
through Kansas, I pray God will take pity
on my aging need to clutch the earth,
and rather than condemn my soul
to everlasting bliss, grant me a little
more in this life than I deserve.

Carolina Wrens

—for Tommy

Silly birds, Mary Oliver called them
for building a nest in a bucket
in a ditch. But imagine my surprise
one fly fishing morning to find
the leg of my waders blocked below
the knee with knitted creek moss,

assorted grasses, tabby fur,
birch bark, and what appeared to be
strands of my wife's golden hair.
I had hung my waders on the porch
to dry, and house wrens spelunked
a yard from bib to shin to build a cradle

for their chicks. Thank god, no eggs
were laid. Beside Pine Creek,
my fly rod close at hand, I pondered
the diligence of wrens as I stretched
to my arm pit to clean nesting
from my boot. What feathered Pluto

would lead his Persephone into such a den,
expect her to incubate young in a darkness
that smelled of feet? The fledglings,
if by some miracle survived,
would tunnel from the underworld
to be blinded by my sunny porch.

The Audubon society says male and female
build nests, that some wrens make twenty nests,
as decoys, seasonal roosts, or to bribe the affection
of their mates, but what I want to know,
oh smallest bird with largest voice, is in what
secret bough you gathered golden hair.

What I Mean to Say

An empty pocket holds something
besides lint. Time, like a ring

with a single key, waits there,
most present in December when

I wear my pockets like gloves.
We sit at the kitchen table and sip

coffee. On this chilled morning,
the first hard frost has hushed

the landscape. The silence between
our words means more to me

than meaning. Meaning, like time,
fills hardwoods with spring leaves

but winter takes them. What I
mean is that most words are like

furniture we use to fill a room
no one sits in. But sometimes

the way words are said comforts
the emptiness. Your hands,

hair curls, and even breaths
soften the darkness, open

mornings with memory,
its pockets, its silences.

An Absence

Sleepless nights I walk the long drive
and listen to my neighbor's mustangs nicker.
The moon catches in their wide eyes

as they come cautiously to the fence
and ask for alfalfa treats. Nothing important
ever happens here when you are away—

raccoons raid the bird feeders,
Belle, the black cat, haunts the porch.
The wind tosses persimmon and gum leaves

that gloss and shimmer above my head.
The morning sun will fire starling feathers,
outline the course of pigeons in flight,

and reveal how a flock forms a single wing
and folds under a bridge. But tonight I'll drift asleep
as stars and dark matter create and order chaos.

I'll wake alone and remember how light breaks across
your sleeping hand, how your palm cradles a life line
so fragile, and for three decades, so close to mine.

Learning to Be Quiet

Learning to be quiet after a semester of talk,
I sit beside the New River, and watch a heron wade
off little island. The heron exists without words.
She relies on stillness, a snag left by April rain,
until she stabs a fish. Agitated by a kingfisher,
she lifts from the water, alights on a sycamore branch,
and scratches the morning with her cry.

I've known this rusty call since childhood.
My brother took me trotline fishing in the Hatchie Bottoms.
One morning as he baited a hook, he drove
a barb in soft flesh between finger and thumb.
I grasped the weighted line that would jerk him
in the snaky water. With his free hand, he clipped
the steel with pliers. I anxiously steered the john boat
between berms as herons lifted from limbs
painting the cypress sky with wings.

Even in meditation the mind strays from mantra
into memory. How easily the cry of a bird leads
to the realm of story. The heron has returned
to her fishing. Like my pulse, she performs
an adagio of measured steps before her posture
settles into sculpture, a note on a staff.

Planet in October

In heat, the neighbor's rottweiler
lunges against her chain.
Three lesser dogs, like Penelope's
suitors, mingle and spar in the yard.
A maple, yellowed with fall,
explodes in the morning sun.
Floyd will turn our old garden soon.
Broken husks of corn, wreckage
of beans will feed migratory doves.
The wood chuck will yawn in layers
of fat and fur. One sunny day
she won't shadow the grassy knoll
beside the wood line. Some mornings
I become a port hole, time splashing
like brine against the pane,
or an opening from which to view
a life so small in the scheme
that I could sit on the porch
and watch shadows change,
listen to red wasps bang the screen,
become acceptable to hummingbirds.
There is little help for a man like me.
I tell the mockingbird not to bother.
She'd rather instruct the cat anyway,
swoop and fuss, alight on a limb
and imitate her version of Babel.
Quiet mornings know all tongues.

IV

Losses

What can anyone give you greater than now,
starting here, right in this room, when you turn around.

—William Stafford

Teaching *Hamlet*

I squint my eyes at first light
sit by the window, and shake
my father's ghost from my dream.
A troubled student hasn't spoken
in days—keeps his head on a table
while his discussion group works.
A friend walks by his desk
and pokes him, whispers in his ear,
only to be shrugged away.
I meet the friend's eyes
as he frowns and shakes his head.

I know what happens to a boy
when he loses a father. After
the funeral, hugs, and the preacher's
words, silence forms an emptiness
in the lungs—breath can be taken in
but not released. I remember
sleepless nights at sixteen,
my brothers and sister tucked away
at college, my mother wracked
with grief. I couldn't stay awake
in school—it was the safe place
to sleep—no scent of Old Spice Aftershave,
no father's coffin face hovering
above the bed when I closed my eyes.

So I'll let Thomas sleep during
Hamlet, and wait for him to come

to me about makeup work.
Don't look for irony in this sketch.
I am not Horatio, nor was meant
to be, and maybe the Danish Prince,
if younger, would have slept in school.

On Hearing that a Friend Has a Week to Live

I finish my coffee, pay the bill,
drive home. Out the window,
the hope of morning brightens gardens
in neighborhood yards. Inside the car

my heart is a silent room in an old house.
Neither sorrow, that easy crutch,
nor prayer, my lonesome companion,
knows the words to this new song.

Only pictures from our last meeting replay:
the cynical jokes about the president,
the anger about the dead, the knowing
nods, careful smiles, and touch of hands.

When Buddhist priests marched across
America for peace, they slept in your basement.
I never asked how they knew to stay
at your house. I want them back

to line the walk to your front door.
Sitting in black robes like sacred crows,
they will hum a chant as hospice workers
leave and the coroner is called. Stones

in your cactus garden will whisper to birds.
Your old cats will hold a wake for friends.
If no one offers, I'll take the tabbies home
and my house won't be as empty as before.

Soliloquy

The cat under my desk is dead,
buried in the back yard, but her
presence still lingers at my feet
or under the rocker, or on the top
stair step when I awaken, drugged
with sleep, go the kitchen,
turn on the coffee. I've hurdled,
fell down steps and tripped
at my desk until she trained me
in one of life's lessons—
watch where you're going.
Once while my wife and I
made love, the cat climbed
on my back for a ride…hard
to stay in the mood, pet clinging
to my shoulders, wife laughing
in my face.

A person can get beat up
in Tennessee for naming a cat
Soliloquy, but that was her name,
always walking around the yard
making speeches to whatever listened.
And when she made a kill—shrew,
titmouse, vole, chipmunk, rat—
she whispered the sweetest song
to each before eating them, starting
with the head, careful to extract
the spleen and gallbladder
on the welcome mat by the door.
Late one night we sat up, startled
from a dead sleep, to hear her

little song coming from the quilt
at our feet. She brought a lizard,
the perfect bed toy, before losing
it beneath our sheets. June bugs,
luna moths, Japanese beetles,
the world was her culinary delight.

When she stopped eating, we knew.
The vet gave us heart meds to rub
in her ears but she hid to keep us at bay.
All hail to the cat who sang like Joni Mitchell,
quoted Lorca and Shakespeare, and was
six pounds of hell on dogs. The softest
foot warmer in catdom…let death
have her now, her old acquaintance.

Prayer for the Newly Dead

—For Ann

Since I assume the dead
no longer pray, I offer
this prayer on your behalf.
Let there be a heaven
with bull frogs in it,
the kind that drum-drummed
Snow Pond and spread
their jellied eggs around
snake grass in the shallows.

An eternal present seems
like hell—let there be a past.
Remember children dancing
in the leaves, Karen and Laura,
their hair bright with sun,
their feet tangled with oak
and sweet gum; your brother
in Vietnam, his letters
told of boys he couldn't save
with a young physician's hands,
and of the boys he could,
how thin he was when
he came home, his smile
a razor. Remember hard years
that kept us close: the flood
of '57 when your father
drove us to watch a chain gang
sandbag the levee, their striped
suits like in an old-time movie.
Barns, cows and tractors

stirred in a Mississippi stew;
a hard freeze, when water receded,
ice-rimmed a thousand cypress trees.

Your floods are over now,
but I'm not sure bliss carries
the weight of heart break.
I pray that little consolations linger:
the taste of sweat, the smell
of tilled soil after rain,
the way morning light
enters a window, the scattered
sound of starlings in the oak
beside the porch, a loved one
napping in another room.

When the Dust Settles

When the dust settles, I'll change my life.
Enough of pawning myself off as some word guru.
I want to greet people at Wal-Mart, drive a forklift,
work at a toll booth, or tend bar in some neighborhood
joint where washed up musicians drink morning beers
and talk about their one big chance. The Nam vet,
who's looked pissed since '69, sits in the corner
where he closes his eyes without dreaming,
listens to the Supremes, and remembers high school
before his life shut, and the Veterans' psychologist
said shell shock instead of delayed stress syndrome,
and pot was cheaper than Prozac.

When the dust settles, I'll own up to things.
My best friend in basic training died in Vietnam,
and I won't search for his name on the black wall.
Though it wasn't my fault, if I stop feeling guilt,
I might forget the love poem Chris wrote to his girl
at Michigan State before being shipped out.
That night some leathernecks roughed me up
when I got drunk and played *Bridge Over Troubled
Water* ten times on the juke box at the bowling alley.

When an orange glow in winter hardwoods signals
morning, and subway commuters seem as lonely
as people in a Hopper painting, I'll walk to the Lincoln
Memorial just to admire the delicate work of those
giant fingers, pass the sculpted metal warriors
with courage stained faces and M-16s. At the wall
I'll look up Christopher W. Christian, who was
so in love in 1968; then review the letters,
cuff links, shaving mugs, and flags left

by grief, loss, love and loneliness. Maybe
I'll cut my lips against the carved black marble
of his name, and whisper something safe and funny
and sacred, I don't know, when the dust settles.

Fall

A word from Old English,
feallan, feol, feallan.
Among its definitions:
to be born,
to lose one's chastity,
Adam's sin, the act
of throwing one's opponent,
a loss of innocence,
the birth of lambs.

Today the mockingbird's
leery tactics—loop the loop
to catch a fly, then chase
the blue bird to the neighbor's barn.
She's not concerned
with autumn's dissolution,
nor the dissonant tremors
wrought by baler, tractor
and wagon to make hay.

Scattered loosestrife
along the pasture edge
sways yellow in October sun
where storm-broken limbs
snag the tree line beside Best Creek.
Widow-makers, my father called them,
when loosened enough to fall.

War loss, a world away,
headlines the news, a soldier

dead from our little town.
Heartbreak visits neighborhood
sidewalks. Willow shadows
on the pond are sickle-shaped.
Fall is the name we give the season.

Rummaging through Causes in the Museum of My Closet

Gathering clothes for Goodwill,
I find an old shoe box full of poems
filled with teenage Marxist angst.
I whistle a little idiot tune while reading
a rant called "After the Revolution
the Poor Will Feed on the Flesh of the Rich."

Saved T-shirts hang in plastic:
Dylan offering a freewheeling smirk,
Lennon with the word, *Imagine*,
Peter, Paul & Mary holding peace signs,
The Who, Fogelberg and Springsteen.
I do a little mental rundown. *The Masters
of War?* They're alive and thriving.
Is *God On Our Side?* The president thinks so,
and if you imagine there's no heaven,
the Christian right will have your job.
The Great Mandala (the wheel of life)
spins precariously at best, justice still
blows in the wind, and too many
brothers live under the bridge.

While we waited for the revolution,
its substitute crept in. My woody
work shirts and parka turned
into Harris tweed and turtlenecks,
my Redwing boots into Docksiders,
my Sears' jeans into Tommy's,
and I teach at the college I protested in.
New wars rage on old battle fields,

religion and politics preach liberty and love,
trump each other for oil and water,
trade food and weapons for power,
and smear citizens with blood.
Old Bob, who's in the watchtower
while we still feed off the lives of the poor?

Prayer for a November Morning

Frost glosses drought grass.
The stray cat waits on the porch
for a handout. The house wren sings
its T-shirt song. The little blue spruce
we planted last Christmas is dying,
needles gone except for one green
branch that reaches out like an orphan.

What do I pray for this morning:
to be a better husband, brother,
teacher? To be kinder, selfless?
For Ray, my neighbor, stationed
north of Bagdad? For families
of the five marines killed Tuesday?
For families of the forty pilgrims
bombed at a burned-out Mosque?
For hurricane victims who lost
their homes and jobs? For under-
standing of terms like *bad intelligence?*
(Dare I say it?) For thousands
maimed in the sweet name of liberty?

I silence late night news
that invaded sleep, and feed
the cat that rubs her face
in my hand. I watch golden
maple leaves shutter in the wind
and bow my head.

Lilies

I have always been late for lilies
that pretend to bloom for a week,
and when my attention wanes,

I find them spoiled by fullness.
It's not that I envy bumblebees
that catch unfurling blossoms

and smother their legs in orange.
I am ripe for perfection: alabaster
smooth and unstained; star gazers,

the rival of orchids; reds as deep
and soft as pinot noir. This
morning a gentle rain whispers

to my garden where lilies wait.
Anticipation is a human disease.
Plants are content as foliage, stems

and buds. The caterpillar, happy
on its feeding rampage, doesn't
rush the dark pain of wings.

Last Rite to the Queen of Grammar

Nothing dangled
when she walked into the room,
not lizards, not participles.
Slang split
but no infinitives.
And pronouns,
objective and subjective,
tap-danced warily
on our tongues.
The minister said,
in confidence,
that she would correct God,
and lawyers sought her out
for conversations.
Churchill would have cowered
behind her use of prepositions,
and Who and Whom felt comfortable
washing and drying supper dishes.
There were stories of how
her father wore his oldest tie
to rake the leaves,
and the mechanic at the ESSO
buttoned his shirt to fill
her tank once a week.
Though we joke about her
on holidays, we write
our checks out to the line,
never mix the second person,
tip precisely, drink scotch neat
on the right occasions,
and proof our children's
thank you notes for spelling.

It is true that we have been unthankful,
that we have been known
to drink white wine with beef,
waste food, curse machines,
and covet our neighbors,
but we don't enjoy it.

My Mother's Soul

My mother looked like a soul
waiting to be surprised. Whether
stirring soup or weeding a garden,
she was fishing for the unexpected,
like the morning at Reelfoot Lake
when her pole bent double,
and she swung a large water snake
swimming the air like a Chinese dragon.
She wouldn't just cut the line
and *throw away a perfectly good hook,*
so I pinned the snake's head,
threaded the barb from its lip,
and released it writhing
and scarred into cypress grass.

My mother wore a slight smile
that posed a question few people
wanted asked, especially the preacher
at Bible study, my sister on the phone,
or my brother sneaking in late
on Saturday night. A soul is what
she looked like until she died,
but forever is a concept I'll leave
to holy men on street corners
holding signs of coming doom.

Give me something concrete,
my mother might have said,
like a snake pumping a fishing line,
or an old woman sailing her death bed
toward the Rapture, her faith strong,
her face like a soul, the morphine "O"
of her mouth dark enough to swallow stars.

My Father Comes to Me

—homage to Mark Strand

All night Heritage Creek roared
a high pitch outside our cabin—
a tropical storm churned
Southern Appalachia.

I dreamed my father took my hand
and said, "Come with me." He led
me to the little cascade where he had
stacked a tower of creek stones
to see how high he could go
before rocks teetered
and splashed in the spray.

His hair wasn't as white as when he died
but his face bore the stress of a man
who balanced a razor inside.
His mouth still held a gentleness.
I had this thought as he took my hand
and led me to the stillness of a moving pool
where he motioned for me to lean
with him over the water, and looking
down, I could see what he meant—
though his eyes were blue and mine brown,
our mouths bore the same tenderness.

"I had to die," he said, "You couldn't save me."
"I know," I said.
"You were only sixteen." he said.
"I know," I said.

"Where have you been," I asked.
"I have been stacking creek stones."
"Where have you been?"
"I have settled in the shadows
of leaves drifting toward decay."

"In what place?
"In our old yard on Sampson Ave."
"In what place?"
"In the memories of your brothers and sister."

"What do you wear?"
"I wear the grease-stained clothes of a mechanic."
"What do you wear?"
"I wear false teeth, a pocket watch and a sailor's smile."

"Why have you come?"
"To show you the shape of our mouths."
"Why have you come?"
"To study light and shadow."

"Did you lie to us?"
"Promises were made."
"Did you lie to us?"
"Silence was my only lie."

"Where will you go?"
"I will walk the pasture with my dogs, Wags and Josephus.
"Where will you go?"
"I will sleep with old house boats on the Tennessee River."

"What will you love?"
"I will always love your mother and you children."
"What will you love?"
"I will love the rain."

"What do you balance inside?"
"Nothing, the dead balance nothing."
"What do you balance inside?"
"Look in the water," he said.

Language of the Hands

When your hands don't know
I'm watching, they sign an inward language,

thumb and forefinger rub together
as if sifting a fine dust—gold, or heart ache,

or soil. The little finger likes to coil
toward the fleshy comfort of the palm,

resting at the edge of a life line
that began in another time, in another

life than this moment of the hand.
See how it likes to cup the chin,

spread fingers around soft cheeks.
The fingertips, those marvels, smooth

the lips which are their closest kin.
Lovers need hands around their faces

and in their hair, want hands to crawl
inside their skin. When you are alone

and don't know I'm watching, your hands
are children of another world, signing

the motion of a private heart, learning slowly
what all hands must—when to let go, what to hold.

V

S‍TORIES

*Assemble first all bits and scraps
Which may make up a world perhaps.*

—Robert Graves

The Secret Lives of Boats

You find canoes in backyards turned upside down
as if they could float the sky, or bass boats
parked in yards covered with plastic, pregnant
with tall seats, or crippled pontoons afloat

in the backwash of rivers, mere skeletons
of their former selves. What contempt they must
have of us who leave our own old and useless,
hulls scarred and rotten, adrift in the storms.

It is true that there are those like my brother
who rescue old canoes, grout and seal the scars,
refit new birch seats and skull them smoothly
on fishing ponds, or my neighbor,

who keeps an ancient sail boat on blocks
to restore the barnacled hull. You can see him
after work painting and polishing wood
to prepare the old lady for one last voyage,

one last feel of water splitting the prow.
How we worship the new chic speed boats
that glare colors and roar their wakes through
floating harbors, jet skis that circle our lakes,

caring little for the depth of life that lurks
beneath the surface. It is rumored among boats
that toss restless in their slips, that ships
still exists that chart the stars, that know

the secret alchemy of moonlight on water,
that speak the language of plankton, and praise
the divinity of whales. There will come a time,
it is said, when tall ships will share waves

with dories, and barges will cruise with skiffs.
One night soon rivers, lakes and oceans will hold
a reborn moon on one surface. Freed from all
moorings, boats will navigate the spheres.

Genesis

A boy from the yellow bus
leaves the dirt road and walks
the short-cut home from school.
On the ridge where pumpkins
grow in seed corn, he picks
the roundest and with a piece
of chalk, draws the Equator
and the Prime Meridian.
With his finger he traces
a spot in the Northern Hemisphere
where a valley marks a river bluff,
and words of his Uncle Randle
rise from that pumpkin to tell
about the woman out berrying,
who got too far from the cabin,
and was caught by the Shawnee,
or a new bride who fell to her death
chasing a swallowtail on a morning
sun-swept of womanhood,
or the young mother walking
home at dusk who was followed
by John Long's son, the quiet
brooding one, who hid his thoughts
from God, who knew in his heart
that he was too low to have
such a woman unless he took her.
She hid her infant in a hollow log
and jumped from the cliff to break
upon the rocks that lined the river.
Even with the boy's few years,
he knows you can't grow enough

pumpkins on that plot to count
the versions of the story. A fiddle
cut the heart, mocked the fate
of the butterfly and Lady's Bluff
marks the map of Perry County.

Green Snake

At willow pond
    a rough green snake,
    gentlest of animals,

blends in perfectly,
    wound like a bracelet
    on an outstretched limb.

Lumped with hoppers,
    it awaits sunlight
    to dapple the leaves.

No Eden here,
    no allegory with an apple,
    just a farm pond,

stocked with bream and catfish,
    home of sliders and bullfrogs
    that the little people pass through

before going under the mountain.
    Young Cherokee don't believe
    in them any more,

 not with boom boxes
    the internet and casinos
    to make them American.

The little people know
    it's good not to exist—
    buried in a book of legends

and small passages of novels.
>   The green snake watches them pass,
>   sticks out its tongue a welcome.

Something Magic,
>   like a crow feather,
>   is left under an oak root

where deeper still a brood
>   of mink are nursing—
>   reminders of the Hopewell,

the stone-box sun worshippers,
>   the mound builders—that 15,000
>   years is a speck of dust.

Oracles

The great horned owl perches like a god
on the oak snag above the porch.
Its yellow eyes, an oracle's, scorch
the night like the eyes of the storefront preacher
in Tennessee where I grew up;
a man so driven to do god's work,
the end being near, the beast peering
over the horizon, that his mob of children
went hungry, did without shoes when
their mother ran off with the Hoover man.
Late one afternoon, he appeared on the roof
of the Court House and railed to heaven
until the sheriff and a fireman
roped him down like a fallen angel.
He spun in the last rays of the delta sun,
hands cuffed behind his back, voice torn,
eyes dancing with a Pentecostal fever.
Six months later he escaped from Central State,
and one chill night, while his children slept
warm and full in the Agape Orphanage,
he burned as his barren chapel torched
the midnight sky with his sacrifice.
Such stories haunt sleepless nights,
while the owl shreds a mole for its
downy brood, then flies back into darkness
chanting its warning like a prayer.

That Story

Some tellers clear their throat
to start a story, some Cherokee
say *this time* and end with *that was
that time.* GrandSally, as a little joke,
started biblically, *and it
came to pass* in a land called
Benton County, one of Jake Long's
sons was squirrel hunting
on a crown of hickory above
the Tennessee River when
a lightening storm drove
him into a cave. In between
thunder claps he heard a sound
he knew from clearing timber,
a din of rattles echoing from
the walls. Without thinking,
he fired his shotgun into
the darkness and pellets
ricocheted in his face. He fell
to the wet floor next to a spring
and washed the powder
and blood from his eyes.
Suddenly chilled, he crawled
to the lip of the cave, gathered
brush and built a fire. He lit
a pine knot and went back
to find the snake. Ten steps in
he found an arrow painted
on the wall pointing down
to a flat shelf where an infant skeleton
wrapped in swaddles stared up

at him, its little bonnet
still tied at the chin.
A few steps further he read
the word *fever* scratched
above a larger child wrapped
in what he thought was horse hide,
and beside it, a cross made of willow
bound with ribbon. In the torch's
flicker, he saw other bundles
measured in steps before a blinding
flash and crash of timber outside
knocked him to the cave floor.
A fisherman found him by the river,
his overalls torn at the knees
from crawling, his eyes swollen shut.
He grasped an ancient ribbon
in his fist. The story came back
to him in sections like remembering
the images of a dream. His brothers
found break down from a rock slide
on the ridge but no cave. All winter
he combed the bluff for the tell-tale
signs of steam drifting from beneath
the ground, but nothing came of it.
He kept the ribbon in his bible
and spoke in tongues in church a lot.

Remains

—For R. C.

The Huff family cemetery in Floyd County
rests on a hill where headstones meet the sky.
I ask Randle why two names, Merit
and Preston Huff, mark one grave.
He clears his throat so I know to pay attention:

These cousins worked
West Virginia coal in 1900.
They stayed late at a barn dance
and were walking to their lodging,
five miles by road, three if they trekked

the railroad tunnel through Iron Mountain.
Neither had a watch but thought
that they could beat the early train.
Half way in narrow granite, the first tremble
had them cracking nervous jokes,

and then the haunting recognition
as the rhythmic rumble entered darkness.
They must have found a terrible silence
of mute screams as the holy spirit entered
their bodies in a din of smoke and light.

An annihilation of hands, feet,
elbows, and knees, their spirits were
snuffed out in night's rapture.
Identities erased, they were shipped home
in a box, buried in the same grave,

the same words spoken over remains.
In the shadow of Buffalo Mountain,
folks that know the story turn in their sleep
when wind roars like a train
or a screech owl whispers, *run from hell.*

Killing Chickens

We hung out on Aunt Black's
back porch, sipped sweet tea
and waited for her to kill
another chicken.
The dumb clucks knew
something was wrong,
but when she scattered
new feed, they'd scurry
from under the shed
to the hard scrabble yard
behind the kitchen. Black
would grab her choice
by the neck and wind
its body in the air like
a cowboy roping a calf.
We wanted to cheer but
her side-glance let us know
that death wasn't funny business.
She killed two when the preacher
was due for dinner; enough
legs, livers, and gizzards for us,
breast and thighs for him.
He talked hell so much
we were glad to eye our food,
thankful for anything.
The only event better than
eating Black's chicken was
watching the killing. Death-flop
my father called it. We'd learn
quick enough Aunt Black warned:
a short headless flight, flapping jumps,
nothing left but the shivers.

Thankful Taylor

> *Dr. J. M. Burger, a practitioner at Murfreesboro, TN,*
> *was called into the case in January, 1874.*

Thankful Taylor didn't know
that she swallowed the snake.
Sipping cool spring water
on a scalding day, she thought
it was a string of grass.
One night she awoke knowing
something alien lived inside her.
A fickle appetite and convulsions
brought the doctor, the minister
and finally a faith healer.
A rhapsody of tongues burned
Pentecostal. When she opened
her mouth to scream, the shadow
of a head appeared in her throat.
For months she fed the serpent
with her meager meals, refreshed
it with well water and gall.
After exhausted fits she slept hard
and dreamed of dark Persephone.
Neighbors said to summon a priest
to drive out Satan, for it was visible
to any one in the room that a beast
rolled in her belly. Thankful feared
she might die without her dismal sister.
In desperation, her mother waited
for the shadow to appear, grabbed it
by the head, and sent for the doctor.
He pulled the snake from her body.
Some say it was bleached white

from stomach acid, the doctor's report:
23 inches and striped brown.
The snake died after separation from its host.
Rumors have it pickled in a jar in some
roadside carnival in Tennessee.
Thankful Taylor would be known
as the Eve, who tempted by the apple,
consumed the serpent. At night, swallowed
by darkness, she shocked awake and stared
through her bedroom window searching for light.

Back Home

He remembers drought as a child,
his grandmother ever watchful of the sky,
his father's silence broken by a shallow cough.

Outside the car, tobacco and corn burn
yellow in the fields. Men in white shirts
stand in oak shade beside a church.

They light each other's smokes,
draw circles of dust with Sunday shoes.
Decoration Day has come and gone,

but every grave is newly clean,
plastic flowers wired to stones,
a worn quilt panel draped on one.

If you see fit is what his father said
to God about the rain, after he blessed
the food his family was *about to eat.*

The words not so different from the breaking
of bread and blood, nor, he imagined,
from tribal prayers a shaman whispered

as blood appeased the fire. He still
thought in farming terms, though
he'd long since left that life behind.

One crop readied kids for school,
one fed the stock, one bought Christmas
if winter wasn't too hard, the bank

breathing down your neck. Mostly
thankful for hard times and good,
they bore a life of quiet anger, quiet joy.

Outside, a crescendo of cicadas,
hum-struck on the cusp of sound,
retreats back toward silence.

On porches, women look to the sky;
men rest on heels, knees bent,
their faces bowed to the ground.

Tennessee Song

How can I give up little night fires
on the Mississippi's cracked sand,
the roll and pitch of the old man,
wood duck's squeal, a flash
of teal in the deep river bends;

how can I give up the mystery of hymns
born from the dark labor of hands,
shot gun shacks, feed troughs, and
floods that hang a back break
of hay in cotton wood limbs;

drought corn roots clutch July soil,
husks touched brown, cobs missing
kernels like toothless grins,
road stench of flattened black snakes,
truck windows flapping the ears of hounds;

how can I not love burned-out trailers
stacked with feed, there use diminished
but not undone, an engine lynched in an oak,
a jake-leg mechanic lowering it down,
a winding of buzzards in the sun;

a clutch of fox bones bleached by moon,
old women spitting snuff in a can,
a sentinel of herons on cypress knees,
a dead tractor honored on a hill top crown,
bee boxes swollen with the labor of bees;

night fires on the rivers cracked sand,
hymns born from the labor of hands,
windows flapping the ears of hounds,
a winding of buzzards in the sky,
a sentinel of herons on cypress knees,
honey in a jar stuffed with cone,
how can I not love all of these?

The Bears

Mountain towns often name
their football teams after animals—
bears, yellow jackets, cougars, bobcats.
Our home team is the Bears.
A meat and three downtown shares
the same name, and old men drink
coffee and brag about the glory days
when the team had a real coach,
and boys with muscular names
like Floyd, Ralf and Harold ran
touchdowns before graduating
to join the Marines or stay home
to work timber. Used to be
a hard working family could
just make it on a farm. Now days
a man and wife clock two shifts
at the factory to eek out a living
and keep what's left of the land
they were raised on. Fast cars that ran
whiskey serve little purpose now
but to race dirt circles or kill
stoned teenagers on weekends.
You can stand on Overlook Mountain
on a fall night and watch football fields
light up for 60 miles down
the Tennessee Valley, hear
the drift of marching bands play
the National Anthem, the bass drums
the only clear cannon salute.
Somewhere in the night, the bears
that run the ridges above hollows
may cock an ear at the valley cheers

before roughing laurel hells to grub
roots on Bob's Bald, where wind
sings to tall grass my father called
the hair of God, and nights still
darken enough to gather stars.

In the Company of Grasses

—For Mary Oliver

All my life
   I have wanted a bedroom
      carpeted with orchard grass

so I could dig my toes
   deep in green, hear the buzz
      of wasps on fallen fruit.

I have been baptized
   breast deep in grasses
      circling my shoulders like water.

They have stroked
   my thighs like the soft
      brush of lovers.

Mountain nights, I have heard
   wind comb a bald of grass
      like the hair of God.

Mountain mornings, grass cradles
   a thousand spider webs
      strung with dew.

In the city grass pokes
   from brick facades
      of old buildings,

forces through cracks
 of weathered concrete where
  traffic and business-talk

collar my dreams,
 knock my heart
  half a bubble off plumb.

Back home, late afternoon,
 I cross the road to unmowed pasture,
  let wheat seed tickle my palm.

In bed by ten, I dream
 grass breathing in the yard,
  its lineage older than bone,
its prayers,
 ancient green,
  singing in darkness.

The Wish

My mother smoked one cigarette each day.
After supper dishes were washed, dried
and put away, she sat on porch steps

and let smoke drift from her perfect mouth
toward a sky so innocent that no one
would guess that it hovered over cities,

mountains and seas. The dreamy look
in her eyes, as street lights flickered on,
might have told a secret, how the warm breeze

that lifted her cotton dress, let it dance
above her knees, reminded her of the ocean
the time she met my father's ship

come back from the war, how a three day
train ride from Memphis to the West Coast
shaped her dreams. She had two young sons,

but didn't know yet of one son's epilepsy,
of another's violent tour in Vietnam,
and of her husband's early death.

Late August, 1946, she held the cigarette
above her head, watched the smoke curl upwards,
then placed it under a rock in the rose garden.

She stared up to the same heavens
that ancient Mayans and Egyptians charted.
Her eyes, safe and soft in the blessed mercy

of the present, found the evening star.
She made a wish, never knowing how
soon or how many times the sky would fall.

My Father Made Love

My father made love to failure.
The curve of his lips turned down
in timid sorrow, to men whose
promises meant little, whose
greed made love to nothing.

My father made love to my mother,
her shoulders, her feet, her hair.
He cherished the air she breathed,
the air that trailed her expectations,
unreached, unreachable.

My father made love to the shower
he crooned in, to the hymns he sang,
to the grape juice he served
as the blood of Jesus, his own
blood mortal and sick in love.

Oh, but cypress knees, birch bark,
arrowheads, igneous rock, tuned motors,
the ears of dogs were his lovers.
My father was the man who made love
to rivers, the Buffalo into the Duck

into the Tennessee. He spread their maps
on the floor and traced their flow
with fingers to read his future.
Cut bait, fishing line, sculling paddle,
the lugger cats he pulled from the water,

he made love to anything. My father
made love to camp sites, to tents he staked
and trenched against the coming rain
when his stars imploded, his mountains folded,
his rivers drown in a desk drawer.

My father died watching *Gun Smoke,*
died loving the carpet I laid him on,
the palms I used to pump his chest,
the lips I placed over his mouth.
His last breath was mine.

In Praise of Winter Trees

A closed heart can't greet
a winter sky. Even a rain puddle
is filled by it, and a horse trough,
and the slow current of creeks.

Winter trees, sycamore and oak,
reach for the sky to offer praise—
stark, hard praise, born from all
those rooted years of bearing

the sky's weight. Some nights
an open heart is filled with vast
spaces between stars the mind
can't grasp. The thought of heaven

is not so much mammothed by
the sky's grandeur, but mystified
beyond our silly notions. Winter
trees aren't arrogant; they praise

no flags, no denominations,
they owe allegiance to the soil.
My sister, when she was younger,
awoke in winter to hold her arms

up to the sky, shiver in the wholeness
of it, let shadows of winter trees
dance sunlight across her face.
Oak, beech, sycamore, maple, and gum,

reenact creation, drop their seeds
from the sky, make their homes
in star dust, and reach back
toward heaven. Trees suffer

drought and freezing rain, accept
the annual tilt toward shorter days.
Some ancient hope, like winter light,
is allied with the gravity of stars.

VI

Coda

Winter Wind Song

> *I only borrowed this dust.*
> —Stanley Kunitz

The sound the wind makes
    circling winter's jagged porch,
    is my father's long whistle
    when he called us home,

a blowing rock in a night storm,
    a mountain bald
    whispering to God,
    my grandmother's eerie lilt—

come-this-away-ka-tee
    as a panther lured
    a girl into the forest
    alone.

Some elemental sound
    still whistles in my dreams,
    wakes me wide-eyed—
    listening, listening

as snow moves in these many years.
    I try to keep the moment,
    stretch it in a solitude
    of lost faces, lost sounds

half hidden in the heart's
    mausoleum.
    There will come a time
    the oracle says at story's start.

Perhaps that time has always been.
   This morning I welcome
   the circling sound
   of winter wind—

a whistle that no longer
   calls me home,
   I wake each morning
   who I am.

Colophon

Bembo was modeled on typefaces cut by Francesco Griffo for Aldus Manutius' printing of *De Aetna* in 1495 in Venice, a book by classicist Pietro Bembo about his visit to Mount Etna. Griffo's design is considered one of the first of the old style typefaces, which include Garamond, that were used as staple text types in Europe for 200 years. Stanley Morison supervised the design of Bembo for the Monotype Corporation in 1929. Bembo is a fine text face because of its well-proportioned letterforms, functional serifs, and lack of peculiarities; the italic is modeled on the handwriting of the Renaissance scribe Giovanni Tagliente. Books and other texts set in Bembo can encompass a large variety of subjects and formats because of its quiet classical beauty and its high readability.

Bill Brown is the author of three chapbooks, three collections of poetry and a writing textbook on which he collaborated with Malcolm Glass. His most recent titles are *Tatters* (MARCH STREET, 2007) and *Gods of Little Pleasures* (SOW'S EAR, 2001). During the past twenty years, he has published hundreds of poems and articles in journals, magazines and anthologies. In 1999 Brown wrote and co-produced the Instructional Television Series, *Student Centered Learning*, for Nashville Public Television. He holds a degree in history from Bethel College and graduate degrees in English from the Bread Loaf School of English, Middlebury College and George Peabody College. For twenty years, Brown directed an award winning writing program at an academic magnet school in Nashville. He retired in 2003 and accepted a part-time lecturer position at Vanderbilt University. In 1995 the National Foundation for Advancement in the Arts named him Distinguished Teacher in the Arts. He has been a Scholar in Poetry at the Bread Loaf Writers Conference, a Fellow at the Virginia Center for the Creative Arts, a two-time recipient of Fellowships in poetry from the Tennessee Arts Commission. He and his wife Suzanne live in the hills north of Nashville with a tribe of cats.

www.ingramcontent.com/pod-product-compliance
Lightning Source LLC
Chambersburg PA
CBHW032125090426
42743CB00007B/470